Reframing Your Reality By Elevating Your Thinking The 90-Day Devotional

David L Jackson III

This book is written for informational purposes only. It contains general thought provoking information. This book is designed to assist with building healthy, strong, and long-lasting partnership, business relationships and a spiritual compass. It is the thoughts, personal and professional opinions of the Author. D. F. G. Publishing House LLC and the Author disclaim any responsibility for actions taken without first seeking professional advice or for misunderstandings on the part of the reader.

D. F. G. Publishing House LLC

J. Cameron International Publishing Boutique LLC

Printed in the United States of America

Book Cover Design: David Jackson III

P. Koffe Brown

ISBN: 979-8-218-52170-7

Dedication

To my beloved family—Cathy, Caryn, David IV, and Christopher—whose unwavering love and grace have been my sanctuary. To the Williams, the Gilliams, and my extended clan, whose support has been my stronghold through the darkest times. And to my aunt, Sandra Kendrick, whose kindness was a beacon when all other lights went out. This book is a testament to the strength you've given me.

To the late Bishop Derrick W. Hutchins, my Father in the Gospel, Teacher, Coach, Mentor, Friend, and Covenant Brother—your wisdom is the foundation upon which I stand. And to Bishop Jerry Wayne Macklin, who embodies the essence of walking the talk—your example is a guiding star.

Acknowledgments

I am deeply grateful for the love and support of my family and friends, whose presence has been a constant source of strength and inspiration. Your grace has been my compass in navigating the storms of life.

I also want to express my heartfelt appreciation to the late Bishop Derrick W. Hutchins Sr. and Bishop Jerry Wayne Macklin. Your guidance and leadership have not only shaped my spiritual journey but have also profoundly influenced the pages of this book.

To all who have been a part of this journey, thank you for helping me elevate my thinking and for contributing, in ways both big and small, to the creation of this work.

'For as he thinks in his heart, so is he.' (Proverbs 23:7a, NKJV).

Contents

Introduction

As the world grappled with the onslaught of the COVID-19 pandemic, I, too, found myself facing daunting mental and physical challenges. It was a time that brought many of us to our knees, questioning our very existence and purpose. But during these trying times, I was introduced to a powerful tool: cognitive reframing. This psychological technique, which involves viewing events, situations, and emotions in a new light, set me on a transformative journey.

While studying the Book of Proverbs, a particular scripture resonated deeply with me: *"For as he thinks in his heart, so is he..."* (Proverbs 23:7, NKJV). This verse echoed the essence of cognitive reframing. It wasn't about denying emotions but understanding that to genuinely change my reality, I had to elevate my thinking.

Elevated thinking wasn't about massive changes but rather consistent, deliberate shifts in perspective. It meant examining every facet of my life and ensuring I embraced only those things that uplifted me and those around me. Challenges still arose, but they no longer imprisoned me.

I share this devotional with you, not as someone standing on a high pedestal but as someone who's been where you are. Someone who's felt the pain, experienced the loss, and faced the daunting challenges. But with a heart full of faith and a mind focused on elevated thinking, I found my way to a better place.

So, as you embark on this journey with me, I encourage you to channel the genuine curiosity of a child; as Jesus once said, *"Let the little children come to me, and do not hinder them, for the kingdom of heaven belongs to such as these."* (Matthew 19:14, NIV).

It's my deepest wish that by the end of this devotional, not only will you find yourself in a better place, but you'll also be equipped with the tools to weather future storms and stay the course. For, in the embrace of elevated thinking and a reframed reality lies limitless potential.

Your Journey Through This Devotional

Welcome to a transformative 90-day journey that invites deep introspection, growth, and a renewed perspective. While the path is laid out day by day, it's crucial to remember that this is your journey. Move at a pace that feels right for you. Here's a brief overview of what to expect:

1. **Daily Premise:** Each day begins with a foundational quote or scripture, setting the tone and theme for that day's reflection.

2. **Illustration:** Through a concise story, analogy, or metaphor, the premise is brought to life, offering a relatable context.

3. **Reflection and Insight:** After each illustration, you'll receive a Reflection and Insight that ties the narrative to the core message. Herein lies the heart of the day's lesson.

4. **Engage Deeply:** Each page is designed for a 3-4 minute read, but the true value is unlocked in the time spent reflecting, enacting the call to action, and connecting with the Father. Two reflection questions will prompt introspection, followed by actionable steps to integrate the lesson into your daily life.

5. **Special Days:** Periodically, you'll encounter special days, like Meditation Day, offering unique activities to enhance your journey. Embrace the guidance, but feel free to adapt the environment or time to best suit your needs.

6. **Document Your Thoughts:** Use the space provided within the devotional to record your responses, feelings, and reflections. This will be a tangible testament to your growth and revelations during this journey.

7. **Feedback and Summary Days:** These days are sprinkled throughout to help you consolidate your learnings, assess your growth, and recalibrate if needed.

8. **Share the Journey:** While this is a personal endeavor, consider sharing insights, challenges, and victories with loved ones. Their perspectives might enrich your experience.

9. **Additional Resource:** A good study Bible can be a valuable companion, offering more profound insights into scriptures and enhancing your understanding.

Remember, while the journey is outlined for 90 days, it's the depth of your engagement, not the speed of completion, that will lead to a genuine transformation. As you venture through these pages, approach each day with childlike curiosity, open-heartedness, and a commitment to elevated thinking.

Here's to reframing your reality!

1
Foundation Of Thought

As we embark on this transformative journey of "Reframing Your Reality by Elevating Your Thinking," it's essential to lay a strong foundation. This week, we will dive deep into the fundamentals of thought and perception. Our thoughts shape our reality more than we realize. By understanding and harnessing the power of our perception, we can set the stage for the profound shifts that the subsequent weeks will introduce. From discerning the power of positive over negative thinking to recognizing the spiritual impact of our thoughts, each day will guide you closer to mastering the art of elevated thinking. Prepare your heart and mind for this week, which will challenge you to view yourself and the world around you in a renewed light.

DAY 1

The Power of Perception

Daily Premise:

"For as he thinks in his heart, so is he."

- Proverbs 23:7.

Illustration: Imagine a glass filled halfway with water. Some view it as half-empty, others as half-full: the same glass, yet two different perceptions. Similarly, in life, two individuals can face the same situation, and one might see it as an insurmountable challenge, while the other is an opportunity to grow. It's not just about the situation; it's about how we perceive it.

Reflection and Insight: Our perceptions, the way we view the world and interpret experiences, have a significant impact on our thoughts, emotions, and actions. We'll feel overwhelmed and stressed if we constantly perceive challenges as threats. But if we view them as opportunities for growth, our mindset shifts. We become more resilient, hopeful, and proactive. It begins by recognizing that our perception is a choice.

Reflection Questions:

1. Think about a recent challenge you faced. How did your perception of the situation affect your reaction?

2. In what areas of your life do you need to shift your perception?

_____

_____

Call to Action: Today, intentionally choose to view a challenge as an opportunity. Whether it's a task at work, a personal goal, or a relationship issue, approach it with a perception of growth and possibility.

Prayer and Reflection: Lord, guide my thoughts and help me see the world through Your eyes. May I not be swayed by negative perceptions but instead find hope and growth in every situation. Grant me the wisdom to recognize the power of my perception and the courage to change it when needed. Amen.

DAY 2

Choosing Positive Over Negative

Daily Premise:

"Finally, brothers and sisters, whatever is true, whatever is noble, whatever is right, whatever is pure, whatever is lovely, whatever is admirable—if anything is excellent or praiseworthy—think about such things."

- Philippians 4:8, NIV.

Illustration: Two seeds were planted side by side. One seed focused on the warmth of the sun and the nourishment of the rain, growing rapidly and blooming in vibrant colors. The other seed lamented the occasional darkness and the infrequent storms, stunting its growth and producing few pale flowers. The environment was the same for both, but their focus determined their outcome.

Reflection and Insight: Our thoughts possess immense power over our well-being and actions. Continually focusing on the negative can drain our energy, demotivate us, and hinder our progress. Conversely, focusing on the positive, even amidst challenges, can uplift our spirit, motivate us, and open doors to opportunities. Recognizing this power, we must actively decide where to direct our attention each day.

Reflection Questions:

1. Reflect on your day or week. What are the positive moments or elements you might have overlooked?

2. How can you actively shift your focus from negative situations to seek out positive aspects or lessons?

_____

_____

_____

_____

Call to Action: Today, make a conscious effort to redirect any negative thoughts. Whenever you catch yourself dwelling on a negative, challenge yourself to find a positive angle or lesson from the situation.

Prayer and Reflection: Heavenly Father, guide my mind to focus on the good, the noble, and the praiseworthy. Strengthen my resolve to choose positivity even when faced with challenges. May I find joy in Your blessings and remain hopeful even in adversity. Amen.

DAY 3

The Role of Faith in Shaping Reality

Daily Premise:

"Now faith is the substance of things hoped for, the evidence of things not seen."

- Hebrews 11:1, NKJV.

Illustration: A man walking through a desert, thirsty and tired, spots an oasis in the distance. While many might dismiss it as a mirage, he believes in its reality, drawing strength from that belief, and eventually reaches the actual oasis. His faith in its existence propelled him forward.

Reflection and Insight: Faith isn't just believing in what we can't see; it's the force that drives us to act even when the odds seem against us. By holding onto faith, we can transform our realities and achieve what might seem impossible.

Reflection Questions:

1. Can you recall a situation where your faith led you to a positive outcome?

2. How does faith shape your daily decisions and actions?

_____

_____

_____

Call to Action: Reflect on an area in your life where you've hesitated. Today, take one step forward in that area, powered by faith.

Prayer and Reflection: Lord, strengthen my faith in You and the path You've set for me. Let my actions be guided by unwavering faith, trusting that all things are possible with You. Amen.

DAY 4

Embracing Change as a Catalyst

Daily Premise:

"Do not conform to the pattern of this world, but be transformed by the renewing of your mind."

- Romans 12:2, NIV.

Illustration: A caterpillar undergoes a transformative process, growing bigger and fundamentally becoming a butterfly. This metamorphosis is not without struggle, but the result is a creature of beauty and freedom.

Reflection and Insight: Though often daunting, change is a catalyst for growth and transformation. By renewing our minds and embracing change, we can rise to new heights and unlock the potential we never knew we had.

Reflection Questions:

1. How do you usually respond to changes in your life?

2. What is one change you can embrace today for personal growth?

_____

_____

_____

Call to Action: Identify an aspect of your life that's remained stagnant. Consider one positive change you can implement to initiate growth.

Prayer and Reflection: Father, grant me the courage to embrace life's changes. May I see them not as obstacles but as opportunities to grow closer to You and the person I'm meant to be. Amen.

DAY 5

Understanding Personal Bias

Daily Premise:

"For now we see through a glass, darkly; but then face to face: now I know in part; but then shall I know even as also I am known."

- 1 Corinthians 13:12, KJV.

Illustration: Two people watch the same movie but have entirely different takes on it. Their personal experiences and biases shaped their interpretations, highlighting the subjective nature of our perceptions.

Reflection and Insight: Every individual carries biases formed by past experiences, teachings, and surroundings. Recognizing these biases helps us understand our reactions and reframe them for a more balanced perspective.

Reflection Questions:

1. Can you identify any personal biases that might be influencing your perceptions?

2. How can you challenge and overcome these biases?

_____

_____

_____

Call to Action: Engage in a conversation with someone who has a different viewpoint than yours. Listen actively and try to understand their perspective without judgment.

Prayer and Reflection: Lord, help me to see beyond my biases and to approach situations and people with an open heart. Grant me the wisdom to discern truth and the humility to learn and grow. Amen.

DAY 6

The Spiritual Impact of Thought

Daily Premise:

"For as he thinks in his heart, so is he."

- Proverbs 23:7, NKJV.

Illustration: Consider a gardener who sows seeds in a plot of land. If he plants flowers, he will see flowers. If he sows weeds, he'll get weeds. The mind is the garden, and our thoughts are the seeds. What we continually think about, we become.

Reflection and Insight: Our thoughts don't just affect our actions; they also resonate with our spirit. Our thoughts influence the spiritual realm, and aligning our thinking with divine principles leads to a harmonious spirit.

Reflection Questions:

1. How do you ensure your thoughts align with your spiritual beliefs?

2. Can you identify moments when positive thinking led to a spiritual revelation?

_____

_____

_____

Call to Action: Today, be mindful of your thoughts. Every time you recognize a negative thought, counteract it with a positive spiritual affirmation.

Prayer and Reflection: Holy Spirit, guide my thoughts to be in harmony with Your will. Let my mind be a vessel of positivity and spiritual alignment. Amen.

DAY 7

The Link Between Thought and Action

Daily Premise:

"Do not be deceived, God is not mocked; for whatever a man sows, that he will also reap."

- Galatians 6:7, NKJV.

Illustration: A craftsman imagines a sculpture in his mind, but until he takes action – chiseling and shaping the marble – his vision remains intangible. The act of creation begins in the mind but manifests through action.

Reflection and Insight: Our thoughts lay the foundation for our deeds. When we continually dwell on certain thoughts, they drive us towards corresponding actions. Thus, by controlling and directing our thoughts, we can influence our life's trajectory.

Reflection Questions:

1. Can you recall a recent instance where your thoughts directly influenced your actions?

2. How do you ensure your actions align with your innermost values and aspirations?

_____

_____

_____

Call to Action: Reflect on a thought or idea you've held onto but never acted upon. Consider one small step you can take today to bring that thought closer to reality.

Prayer and Reflection: Lord, let my actions reflect the purity and positivity of my thoughts. Grant me the strength to act in alignment with Your purpose for me. Amen.

DAY 8

Meditation Day: Mindful Awareness

Guided Meditation:

1. Sit in a quiet place, free from distractions.

2. Close your eyes and take a deep breath.

3. As you breathe out, release any tension.

4. Visualize a calm lake, its surface smooth and undisturbed.

This lake represents your mind. Every thought is like a ripple. Watch the ripples, acknowledge them without judgment, and let them disappear. Dive deeper into the stillness, allowing yourself to be fully present.

Reflection: How did the meditation make you feel? Were you able to observe your thoughts without attachment?

Call to Action: Dedicate 10 minutes daily to mindful meditation. As you practice, notice how this mindfulness permeates other aspects of your life.

Prayer and Reflection: God, in the silence of my heart, I find You. As I meditate and become more mindful, guide me to a deeper understanding of Your love and presence in my life. Amen.

2

Overcoming Challenges

As we transition, our journey takes a turn towards the inevitable hurdles and challenges life throws our way. While our foundational thoughts shape our perceptions, how we approach and overcome challenges truly tests our growth and resilience. This week, we'll explore the art of seeing obstacles as opportunities and the role of faith in guiding us through tumultuous times. From understanding the significance of resilience to drawing inspiration from biblical overcomers, we aim to equip you with the tools and mindset to rise above adversities. Ready yourself not just to face but embrace challenges with newfound strength and perspective. The road ahead may have its bumps, but with faith and perseverance, you'll learn to navigate it gracefully.

DAY 9

Transforming Obstacles into Opportunities

Daily Premise:

"Consider it pure joy, my brothers and sisters, whenever you face trials of many kinds, because you know that the testing of your faith produces perseverance."

- James 1:2-3, NIV.

Illustration: Thomas Edison made 1,000 unsuccessful attempts at inventing the light bulb. When asked about it, Edison said, "I didn't fail 1,000 times. The light bulb was an invention with 1,000 steps."

Reflection and Insight: Every challenge you face is an opportunity for growth. Instead of viewing obstacles as setbacks, see them as lessons that propel you closer to your goals.

Reflection Questions:

1. Think about a recent challenge. What lesson did it teach you?

2. How can you shift your perspective to see obstacles as opportunities?

_____

_____

_____

Call to Action: Today, write down three perceived "failures" or "setbacks" and reframe them as lessons learned or steps toward success.

Prayer and Reflection: Lord, grant me the wisdom to see Your guidance in every challenge and the perseverance to transform obstacles into stepping stones. Amen.

DAY 10

Facing Fears with Faith

Daily Premise:

"For God has not given us a spirit of fear, but of power and of love and of a sound mind."

- 2 Timothy 1:7, NKJV.

Illustration: A young bird, hesitant to leave its nest for the first time, is unsure of its ability to fly. With encouragement and trust in its innate abilities, it takes the leap and soars.

Reflection and Insight: Fear can hold us back from achieving our true potential. With faith as our foundation, we can confront and overcome our deepest fears.

Reflection Questions:

1. What fears are currently holding you back?
2. How can your faith guide you in confronting these fears?

_____

_____

_____

Call to Action: Identify one fear you'd like to confront. Pray about it and take one small step to address it today.

Prayer and Reflection: Divine Protector, in You, I find my strength. Help me to face my fears with unwavering faith, knowing You are beside me. Amen.

DAY 11

The Role of Resilience

Daily Premise:

"But those who hope in the LORD will renew their strength. They will soar on wings like eagles; they will run and not grow weary, they will walk and not be faint."

- Isaiah 40:31, NIV.

Illustration: A bamboo tree can bend under the weight of a storm but rarely breaks. Once the storm passes, it returns to its upright position, demonstrating its resilience.

Reflection and Insight: Life's challenges test our strength and resolve. Resilience isn't about avoiding struggles but emerging stronger after facing them.

Reflection Questions:

1. Can you recall a time when you demonstrated resilience?

2. How does your faith contribute to your ability to bounce back from setbacks?

_____

_____

_____

Call to Action: Reflect on a challenge you're currently facing. Write down three strategies, grounded in your faith, that can help you navigate it resiliently.

Prayer and Reflection: God of strength, imbue me with resilience to weather life's storms, drawing inspiration from Your unwavering presence. Amen.

DAY 12

The Inspiration of Overcomers in Scripture

Daily Premise:

"I have told you these things so that in me you may have peace. In this world, you will have trouble. But take heart! I have overcome the world."

- John 16:33, NIV.

Illustration: From Joseph, who rose to power after being sold into slavery, to Esther, who courageously saved her people, the Bible is replete with individuals who overcame immense challenges.

Reflection and Insight: Scripture offers timeless lessons on perseverance, courage, and trust in God. These narratives can inspire us in our personal journeys of overcoming.

Reflection Questions:

1. Which biblical character's story of overcoming resonates with you the most?

2. What specific attributes or actions of this character can you emulate in your life?

_____

_____

_____

Call to Action: Choose a biblical story of an overcomer. Spend some time today reading and reflecting on it, drawing strength and inspiration.

Prayer and Reflection: Lord of History, as I delve into Your Word, let me draw inspiration from the lives of those who trusted in You and overcame. May their stories bolster my faith. Amen.

DAY 13

Embracing Failure as a Stepping Stone

Daily Premise:

"For though the righteous fall seven times, they rise again."

- Proverbs 24:16, NIV.

Illustration: Consider a child learning to walk. Each fall, each stumble, is not a sign of failure but a step toward mastering the skill of walking.

Reflection and Insight: Every failure is an opportunity for growth. Embracing this mindset allows us to learn, adapt, and move closer to our goals.

Reflection Questions:

1. How do you typically react to failure?
2. How can you change your perspective to see failure as a learning opportunity?

_____

_____

_____

Call to Action: Reflect on a recent failure or setback. Write down what you learned from it and how it can guide your future actions.

Prayer and Reflection: Teach me, O Lord, to see failures not as dead-ends but as pathways leading to growth and maturity. Amen.

DAY 14

Moving Beyond Limiting Beliefs

Daily Premise:

"I can do all things through Christ who strengthens me."

- Philippians 4:13, NKJV.

Illustration: An elephant, when young and chained to a post, believes it cannot break free. As it grows, even a thin rope can hold it, not because of its strength but due to its limiting belief.

Reflection and Insight: Our beliefs can empower or restrict us. We can break free from self-imposed constraints by identifying and challenging limiting beliefs.

Reflection Questions:

1. What limiting beliefs might be holding you back?

2. How can your faith help you to challenge and overcome these beliefs?

_____

_____

_____

Call to Action: Identify one limiting belief you hold. Pray about it and seek scriptural or spiritual guidance to challenge it.

Prayer and Reflection: God of possibilities, free me from the chains of limiting beliefs. Let Your truth guide me to see the boundless potential You've instilled in me. Amen.

DAY 15

Visual Day: Inspirational Imagery of Overcoming

Introduction: Visual imagery has the power to evoke deep emotions and inspire action. Today, we'll immerse ourselves in images that symbolize overcoming challenges, drawing strength and motivation from their powerful narratives.

Suggested Imagery:

1. **A Mountain Climber** reaching the peak after a strenuous ascent, signifying the rewards of persistence.

2. **A Blooming Flower** amidst cracked, dry earth, symbolizing hope and resilience in adversity.

3. **A Bridge** spanning a vast canyon, illustrating the power of connection and unity in overcoming obstacles.

4. **A Butterfly** emerging from its cocoon, representing transformation and new beginnings.

Reflection Questions:

1. Which image resonates with you the most and why?

2. Can you recall a time in your life when you experienced a similar form of overcoming?

Call to Action: Spend some quiet moments today visualizing yourself in these scenes of overcoming. Feel the emotions, harness the strength, and let it invigorate your spirit.

Prayer and Reflection: Creator of all beauty, as I meditate on these images of triumph and perseverance, infuse my spirit with the same resilience and determination. Let these visuals be a reminder of Your promise to see me through every challenge. Amen.

3

Relationship And Connections

Let's examine the intricate tapestry of relationships and connections that enrich our lives. As social beings, the bonds we form profoundly influence our thoughts, emotions, and actions. This week, we'll explore the beauty of meaningful connections, the healing power of detaching from toxic ties, and the significance of setting healthy boundaries. Drawing inspiration from scriptural wisdom, we'll reflect on the essence of Christ-like interactions and the joy of nurturing a profound connection with the Divine. Prepare to introspect, celebrate, and fortify the relationships that sculpt your reality. Embrace this opportunity to foster bonds that uplift and guide you closer to your spiritual core.

DAY 16

The Influence of Company on Thought

Daily Premise:

"Do not be misled: 'Bad company corrupts good character."

– 1 Corinthians 15:33, NIV.

Illustration: Consider a boat that, when tethered to a heavy anchor, struggles to move forward despite the strength of its engine. The company we keep can similarly either anchor or propel us.

Reflection and Insight: The people around us significantly influence our thoughts, actions, and even our destiny. Associating with positive, uplifting individuals can propel us towards our goals.

Reflection Questions:

1. Who in your life acts as a positive influence?

2. Are there relationships that feel like they're holding you back?

_____

_____

_____

Call to Action: Evaluate your current relationships and consider if they align with your spiritual and personal growth journey.

Prayer and Reflection: Lord, grant me the wisdom to recognize the influence of those around me and the strength to foster relationships that uplift and inspire. Amen.

DAY 17

Building Bonds that Elevate

Daily Premise:

"As iron sharpens iron, so one person sharpens another."

- Proverbs 27:17, NIV.

Illustration: Two musicians, practicing separately, can create lovely tunes. However, when collaborating, they can produce a harmonious duet that elevates the entire performance.

Reflection and Insight: In life, creating strong, supportive bonds with others can elevate both parties involved, leading to mutual growth and development.

Reflection Questions:

1. How have collaborative relationships elevated your personal or spiritual journey?

2. What qualities do you value in relationships that foster growth?

_____

_____

_____

Call to Action: Reach out to someone today and express gratitude for how they've supported or uplifted you.

Prayer and Reflection: Heavenly Father, thank You for placing individuals in my life who uplift and challenge me. May I also be a beacon of support to others. Amen.

DAY 18

Healing from Toxic Connections

Daily Premise:

"Cast all your anxiety on Him because He cares for you."

- 1 Peter 5:7, NIV.

Illustration: A tree with a parasitic vine may wither, but once the vine is removed, it can regain its strength and grow.

Reflection and Insight: Toxic relationships can drain us emotionally and spiritually. Identifying and healing from such connections is essential for our well-being.

Reflection Questions:

1. Have you experienced a relationship that felt draining or toxic?

2. What steps can you take to heal and protect your emotional and spiritual well-being?

_____

_____

_____

Call to Action: Consider setting boundaries or seeking counseling to address and heal from toxic relationships.

Prayer and Reflection: God of healing, guide me away from connections that harm my spirit and lead me towards those that nurture my growth. Amen.

DAY 19

Understanding Boundaries

Daily Premise:

"Above all else, guard your heart, for everything you do flows from it."

- Proverbs 4:23, NIV.

Illustration: A garden with a fence isn't built to keep beauty in but to keep pests out, ensuring the plants inside thrive.

Reflection and Insight: Setting boundaries is a form of self-care. Determining what we allow into our lives and what we choose to keep out is essential.

Reflection Questions:

1. Where might you need to establish stronger boundaries in your life?

2. How do boundaries align with self-care and respect?

_____

_____

_____

Call to Action: Evaluate an area of your life where boundaries may be lacking and take one step towards establishing a more explicit limit.

Prayer and Reflection: Lord, grant me the wisdom to set boundaries that protect and nurture my spirit, mind, and body. Amen.

DAY 20

Reflecting Christ in Interactions

Daily Premise:

"Let your light shine before others, so that they may see your good works and give glory to your Father who is in heaven."

- Matthew 5:16, ESV.

Illustration: A lighthouse stands tall, guiding ships in the darkest nights, reflecting the safety of the shore.

Reflection and Insight: By embodying Christ's teachings in our interactions, we can be a beacon of hope, love, and understanding to others.

Reflection Questions:

1. How can you more clearly reflect Christ's love in your daily interactions?

2. When have you felt Christ's love through someone else's actions?

_____

_____

_____

Call to Action: Today, make a conscious effort to reflect the love of Christ in at least one interaction you have.

Prayer and Reflection: Jesus, help me to reflect Your love, grace, and understanding in every interaction. Let me be a beacon of Your light in this world. Amen.

DAY 21

Nurturing Connection with the Divine

Daily Premise:

"But whenever you pray, go into your room and shut the door and pray to your Father who is in secret; and your Father who sees in secret will reward you."

- Matthew 6:6, NRSV.

Illustration: A plant, when nurtured with sunlight, water, and nutrients, grows strong and blooms beautifully. Similarly, our spiritual connection thrives with regular nurturing.

Reflection and Insight: Nurturing our connection with the Divine through prayer, meditation, and study allows us to grow spiritually and stay grounded.

Reflection Questions:

1. How do you currently nurture your connection with the Divine?

2. Are there new spiritual practices you'd like to explore?

_____

_____

_____

Call to Action: Set aside a specific time each day this week to focus on nurturing your connection with the Divine, be it through prayer, meditation, or study.

Prayer and Reflection: Divine Creator, help me to consistently nurture my connection with You, drawing strength, guidance, and peace from our relationship. Amen.

DAY 22

Meditation Day: Loving Kindness

Introduction: Meditation has the power to transform the mind and heart. Today, immerse yourself in a Loving Kindness Meditation, extending love and well wishes to yourself and others.

Guided Meditation:

1. Start by sitting comfortably, closing your eyes, and taking deep breaths.

2. Begin by sending love to yourself: *"May I be happy, may I be well, may I be safe, may I be peaceful and at ease."*

3. Think of someone you love and send them the same wishes.

4. Consider someone you're neutral about, and extend your wishes.

5. Think of someone you have difficulty with, and extend your wishes.

6. Conclude by extending these wishes to all beings everywhere.

Reflection Questions:

1. How did it feel to send loving kindness to different people, especially those you might have conflicts with?

2. How can this meditation impact your day-to-day interactions?

_____

_____

Call to Action: Practice this Loving Kindness Meditation daily to cultivate love and understanding in your heart.

Prayer and Reflection: God of Love, as I practice this meditation, help me to genuinely extend love and kindness to all, reflecting Your boundless love. Amen.

4

Growth And Transformation

O ur focus shifts to the transformative power of growth, a subtle and profound journey. Growth isn't just about significant leaps; it often manifests in the small, daily evolutions of our thoughts and actions.

This week, we'll explore the nuances of personal development, celebrating every victory, be it minute or monumental. Through scriptural teachings on renewal and the science of habits, we'll gain insights into the continuous cycle of becoming and evolving. Let this week testify to your resilience, adaptability, and potential. Embrace the metamorphosis, for in each moment of growth, there lies an opportunity to move closer to the best version of yourself.

DAY 23

Embracing Personal Growth

Daily Premise:

"And we all, with unveiled face, beholding the glory of the Lord, are being transformed into the same image from one degree of glory to another."

- 2 Corinthians 3:18, ESV.

Illustration: A caterpillar undergoes a challenging process within its cocoon, emerging as a beautiful butterfly. This transformation isn't immediate, but the result is worth the journey.

Reflection and Insight: Personal growth often comes with challenges, but embracing the process leads to transformation and a higher version of oneself.

Reflection Questions:

1. In what areas of your life have you experienced significant growth?

2. What challenges have shaped and refined you?

_____

_____

_____

Call to Action: Identify one area of your life in which you'd like to grow and take a small step towards that growth today.

Prayer and Reflection: Lord, guide me through my growth journey, giving me the strength to embrace challenges and the vision to see the beauty of transformation. Amen.

DAY 24

Celebrating Small Victories

Daily Premise:

"Do not despise these small beginnings, for the Lord rejoices to see the work begin..."

- Zechariah 4:10, NLT.

Illustration: A magnificent castle wasn't built in a day. Each brick laid is a testament to progress and a step closer to the grand vision.

Reflection and Insight: While it's essential to have big goals, celebrating small victories along the way keeps us motivated and acknowledges our progress.

Reflection Questions:

1. What small victories have you recently achieved?

2. How can you better recognize and celebrate these moments?

_____

_____

_____

Call to Action: Take a moment today to celebrate a recent small victory, no matter how minor it might seem.

Prayer and Reflection: Father, help me recognize and celebrate every step of progress, understanding that each victory, big or small, brings me closer to Your purpose for me. Amen.

DAY 25

The Butterfly Effect on Personal Development

Daily Premise:

"And let us not grow weary of doing good, for in due season we will reap if we do not give up."

- Galatians 6:9, English Standard Version, ESV.

Illustration: The flap of a butterfly's wings can cause a tornado miles away, as per the Butterfly Effect theory. Similarly, small actions in our personal development can lead to significant changes in our lives.

Reflection and Insight: Tiny, consistent steps in personal development can result in profound transformations over time.

Reflection Questions:

1. How have small actions or decisions led to significant changes in your life?

2. What small step can you commit to daily to facilitate growth?

_____

_____

_____

Call to Action: Identify one small habit or action to implement daily, understanding its potential for significant transformation over time.

Prayer and Reflection: Lord, grant me the patience and perseverance to commit to small, consistent actions, trusting in their potential for profound transformation. Amen.

DAY 26

Scriptural Teachings on Renewal

Daily Premise:

"Therefore, if anyone is in Christ, he is a new creation. The old has passed away; behold, the new has come."

- 2 Corinthians 5:17, English Standard Version, ESV.

Illustration: A potter takes a flawed pot, reshapes it, and creates a new, beautiful vessel. Similarly, through our faith and experiences, we undergo a renewal process.

Reflection and Insight: Scripture teaches that with faith and a relationship with Christ, we can experience spiritual and personal renewal, leaving behind the old and embracing the new.

Reflection Questions:

1. How have you experienced renewal in your faith journey?

2. In what areas of your life are you seeking renewal?

_____

_____

_____

Call to Action: Spend time in prayer and reflection, seeking guidance on areas where you desire renewal.

Prayer and Reflection: Heavenly Father, renew my spirit and mind, guiding me towards a transformed life that aligns with Your will and purpose. Amen.

DAY 27

The Science of Habits

Daily Premise:

"Whatever you have learned or received or heard from me, or seen in me—put it into practice. And the God of peace will be with you."

- Philippians 4:9, NIV.

Illustration: Just as water flows through a path of least resistance, our brains form pathways through repeated actions, leading to habits.

Reflection and Insight: Neuroscience shows that repeated actions form neural pathways, making habits automatic over time. Understanding this can help us create positive habits and replace negative ones.

Reflection Questions:

1. What positive habits would you like to cultivate?

2. Which negative habits do you wish to replace, and how can understanding the science of habits help in this process?

_____

_____

_____

Call to Action: Choose one positive habit to cultivate. Commit to practicing it daily, understanding that this repeated action can become second nature over time.

Prayer and Reflection: God, give me the strength and discipline to cultivate positive and replace negative habits, leading me closer to Your design for my life. Amen.

DAY 28

Setting Intentions for Evolution

Daily Premise:

"Many are the plans in a person's heart, but it is the Lord's purpose that prevails."

- Proverbs 19:21, NIV.

Illustration: A gardener doesn't just plant seeds haphazardly. They set clear intentions by planning, preparing the soil, and choosing the right seeds for the desired outcome.

Reflection and Insight: In our growth journey, setting clear intentions aligned with our faith and purpose can guide our evolution.

Reflection Questions:

1. What intentions have you set for your personal growth?

2. How do these intentions align with your faith and purpose?

_____

_____

_____

Call to Action: Set or revisit a clear intention for your personal and spiritual evolution, ensuring it aligns with your faith and God-given purpose.

Prayer and Reflection: Lord, as I set my intentions, may they align with Your purpose for my life, guiding my steps in growth and transformation. Amen.

DAY 29

Visual Day: Symbols of Growth

Activity: Today, take a visual journey. Look for symbols of growth around you - whether it's a budding flower, a growing child, or a building under construction. Capture these symbols through photos or sketches.

Reflection and Insight: Visual symbols are potent reminders of our growth journey. They remind us of the beauty and potential inherent in every stage of development.

Reflection Questions:

1. What symbols of growth did you observe?

2. How do these symbols relate to your growth journey?

_____

_____

_____

_____

Call to Action: Create a visual journal or mood board with your identified symbols. Refer to it regularly as a source of inspiration and reminder of your growth journey.

Prayer and Reflection: Creator God, as I observe symbols of growth around me, may I be reminded of the potential within me and Your continuous work in my life. Amen.

DAY 30

Feedback Day: Reflection on Growth

Activity: Take a moment to reflect on your journey through this week's devotional. Write down your insights, challenges, victories, and areas where you've grown.

Reflection and Insight: Feedback and reflection are vital in assessing our growth and setting our path forward.

Reflection Questions:

1. How has this week's devotional influenced your perspective on growth and transformation?

2. In what areas have you noticed growth, and where do you feel you need further development?

_____

_____

_____

_____

Call to Action: Share your reflections with a trusted friend or mentor, seeking their insights and feedback to guide your journey further.

Prayer and Reflection: God of Growth, thank You for the insights and transformations I've experienced this week. Continue to guide my journey, and may I always be open to growth in Your grace. Amen.

5

The Future And Vision

L et's pivot our gaze towards the horizon, where dreams unfold and visions crystallize. The future is not just a distant realm; it's a canvas colored by our beliefs, hopes, and proactive steps taken today.

This week, we will delve into the artistry of creating a vision, harnessing the potent blend of imagination and faith. By aligning with divine guidance and sidestepping the pitfalls of instant gratification, we chart a course brimming with purpose and potential. As we journey through each day, let's challenge ourselves to dream bigger, seek signs, and craft a vision that resonates with our spiritual core. In the dance between the now and the next, may you find clarity, inspiration, and a future illuminated by divine light.

DAY 31

Crafting a Vision Aligned with Faith

Daily Premise:

"For we walk by faith, not by sight."

- 2 Corinthians 5:7, NIV.

Illustration: Imagine a master builder. Before constructing a building, they craft a blueprint—a vision—that guides each step. Likewise, with faith as our foundation, we, too, can craft a vision for our lives.

Reflection and Insight: Your faith can be the cornerstone of your vision, guiding you toward a future that aligns with God's purpose for you.

Reflection Questions:

1. How does your faith influence your vision for the future?
2. How can you better align your vision with God's purpose for your life?

_____

_____

_____

Call to Action: Create a vision board or journal entry that aligns with your faith and desired future.

Prayer and Reflection: Lord, guide me in crafting a vision for my life that is in harmony with Your purpose. Amen.

DAY 32

The Power of Visualization

Daily Premise:

"For the things which are seen are temporary, but the things which are not seen are eternal."

- 2 Corinthians 4:18, NIV.

Illustration: Consider an athlete preparing for a race, visualizing each step, each breath, and crossing the finish line. This mental preparation helps them achieve their goal.

Reflection and Insight: Visualization isn't just imagining outcomes; it's a powerful tool to manifest one's faith and bring about desired results aligned with that faith.

Reflection Questions:

1. How have you used visualization in your life?

2. How can you incorporate faith into your visualization practices?

_____

_____

_____

Call to Action: Spend 10 minutes visualizing a goal you want to achieve while aligning it with your faith.

Prayer and Reflection: Heavenly Father, grant me clarity in my visions and align them with Your will. Amen.

DAY 33

Embracing Divine Guidance in Plans

Daily Premise:

"A man's heart plans his way, But the Lord directs his steps."

- Proverbs 16:9, NIV.

Illustration: A ship's captain sets a course, but the compass and stars guide him. While we might develop plans in our life journey, God's guidance truly directs us.

Reflection and Insight: Though we make plans, being open to God's guidance ensures our journey is purposeful and fulfilling.

Reflection Questions:

1. Can you recall a time when your plans changed due to divine intervention?

2. How do you remain open to God's guidance when making plans?

_____

_____

_____

Call to Action: Seek God's guidance through prayer and scripture reading in your current plans.

Prayer and Reflection: Lord, let me embrace Your guidance in all my endeavors, knowing Your direction is always best. Amen.

DAY 34

The Danger of Short-term Gratification

Daily Premise:

"And the world is passing away along with its desires, but whoever does the will of God abides forever."

- 1 John 2:17, NIV.

Illustration: Think of Esau, who, in a moment of hunger, traded his birthright for a bowl of stew. The allure of immediate gratification often closes our eyes to long-term rewards.

Reflection and Insight: By aligning our desires with God's will, we can overcome the temptations of short-term gratification and focus on eternal rewards.

Reflection Questions:

1. What short-term gratifications challenge you the most?

2. How can your faith help you prioritize long-term rewards?

_____

_____

_____

Call to Action: List down temptations of short-term gratifications and contrast them with the long-term benefits of resisting them.

Prayer and Reflection: Lord, grant me the strength to prioritize eternal rewards over fleeting pleasures. Amen.

DAY 35

Paving the Path to Purpose

Daily Premise:

"For we are his workmanship, created in Christ Jesus for good works, which God prepared beforehand, that we should walk in them."

- Ephesians 2:10, NIV.

Illustration: A potter shapes clay into a vessel, each touch intentional and purposeful. God, our Divine Potter, shapes our lives with a specific purpose.

Reflection and Insight: By understanding God's purpose for us, we can align our paths to fulfill His divine intentions.

Reflection Questions:

1. How do you see God's purpose unfolding in your life?

2. What steps can you take to better align with this divine purpose?

Call to Action: Reflect on God's purpose for your life and set actionable steps to walk in that purpose.

Prayer and Reflection: God, guide me to understand my purpose and provide me the strength to walk in it. Amen.

DAY 36

Recognizing Divine Signs

Daily Premise:

"Ask, and it will be given to you; seek, and you will find; knock, and it will be opened to you."

- Matthew 7:7, NIV.

Illustration: Imagine a traveler lost in a forest, but occasionally, they see markers pointing the way out. In life, God provides signs, sometimes subtle, guiding us on our journey.

Reflection and Insight: Being attuned to God's signs can lead us to the right path and decisions aligned with His will.

Reflection Questions:

1. Can you recall a time you recognized a divine sign?

2. How can you become more attuned to recognizing God's guidance?

_____

_____

_____

Call to Action: Spend time in silent reflection, seeking and acknowledging God's signs in your life.

Prayer and Reflection: Lord, open my eyes to recognize the signs You place in my path and grant me the wisdom to follow them. Amen.

DAY 37

Meditation Day: Envisioning the Future

Guidance:

1. Sit quietly and breathe deeply.

2. Visualize your future as guided by God's hand.

3. See the path unfolding, filled with purpose, growth, and fulfillment.

4. Trust in God's vision for your life.

Prayer and Reflection: Lord, as I meditate on the future, let Your divine vision guide my thoughts and emotions. Help me trust in Your perfect plan for me. Amen.

_____

_____

_____

6

Gratitude And Contentment

We will immerse ourselves in the profound realms of gratitude and contentment. These aren't just emotions; they are powerful states of being that can reshape our outlook and enrich our lives.

This week, we'll explore the transformative impact of acknowledging our blessings, no matter how small, and finding a deep sense of satisfaction in our present moments. Scripture reminds us of the importance of a grateful heart, and through this journey, we will discover how gratitude acts as a bridge from scarcity to abundance.

As each day unfolds, let's endeavor to find joy in the mundane, radiate thankfulness, and let the ripples of our gratitude touch the lives of those around us. In this sacred dance of appreciation and contentment, may you discover an ever-flowing wellspring of peace and joy.

DAY 38

The Daily Act of Counting Blessings

Daily Premise:

"Give thanks in all circumstances; for this is God's will for you in Christ Jesus."

- 1 Thessalonians 5:18, NIV.

Illustration: A woman kept a gratitude jar where she'd write down something she was thankful for each day. By year's end, she realized even on tough days, there was always a blessing to acknowledge.

Reflection and Insight: Daily gratitude transforms our perspective, making us aware of God's continuous blessings, big or small.

Reflection Questions:

1. What blessings did you recognize today?
2. How has gratitude changed your perspective on difficult days?

_____

_____

_____

Call to Action: Start a gratitude journal, noting down at least one blessing daily.

Prayer and Reflection: Lord, thank You for Your daily blessings. Help me recognize and appreciate them every day. Amen.

DAY 39

Finding Contentment in the Present

Daily Premise:

"I have learned to be content whatever the circumstances."

- Philippians 4:11b, NIV.

Illustration: Imagine a child playing in the rain, finding joy in every drop, regardless of the storm. Like the child, we can find contentment in every moment, trusting God's plan.

Reflection and Insight: Contentment doesn't mean complacency but recognizing and appreciating God's presence in every situation.

Reflection Questions:

1. In what situations do you struggle to find contentment?

2. How can faith guide you toward contentment in those moments?

_____

_____

_____

Call to Action: Reflect on a challenging situation and identify elements where you can find contentment.

Prayer and Reflection: Father, guide me to find contentment in every situation, trusting in Your divine plan. Amen.

DAY 40

Scriptural Teachings on Gratitude

Daily Premise:

"O give thanks unto the Lord; for he is good; for his mercy endureth forever."

- 1 Chronicles 16:34, KJV.

Illustration: In ancient times, after a bountiful harvest, communities would gather to give thanks for their blessings. This wasn't just about the crops but gratitude for God's provision.

Reflection and Insight: Scriptures emphasize the importance of gratitude, teaching us always to acknowledge God's hand in our lives.

Reflection Questions:

1. How do scriptural teachings on gratitude resonate with you?

2. How can you incorporate these teachings into daily life?

_____

_____

_____

Call to Action: Choose a scriptural verse on gratitude and meditate on it this week.

Prayer and Reflection: Lord, instill in me a grateful heart, always acknowledging Your provision and love. Amen.

DAY 41

The Mental Shift from Scarcity to Abundance

Daily Premise:

"The thief comes only to steal and kill and destroy; I came that they may have life, and have it abundantly."

- John 10:10, NIV.

Illustration: Two people view a glass of water: one sees it half-empty, the other half-full. Our perspective on life can be similar, either focused on scarcity or abundance.

Reflection and Insight: With faith, we can shift our mindset from one of lack to recognizing God's abundant blessings in our lives.

Reflection Questions:

1. In what areas do you focus on scarcity?
2. How can faith help you see abundance?

_____

_____

_____

Call to Action: List areas of perceived scarcity in your life, and next to them, note down potential blessings or areas of abundance.

Prayer and Reflection: God, help me shift my perspective, recognizing the abundance You provide in my life. Amen.

DAY 42

Embracing Joy in the Mundane

Daily Premise:

"This is the day the Lord has made; let us rejoice and be glad in it."

- Psalm 118:24, NIV.

Illustration: A monk found joy in every chore, from sweeping to washing dishes. He saw each as a moment to connect with God, transforming mundane tasks into acts of worship.

Reflection and Insight: Finding joy in everyday tasks is a way to acknowledge God's presence in every moment of our lives.

Reflection Questions:

1. Which mundane tasks feel most tedious to you?

2. How can you find joy in them?

_____

_____

_____

Call to Action: Choose a routine task and approach it with mindfulness and joy, seeing it as an act of worship.

Prayer and Reflection: Lord, help me find joy in every moment, seeing Your hand in even the most mundane tasks. Amen.

DAY 43

The Ripple Effect of Gratitude

Daily Premise:

"And let the peace of Christ rule in your hearts, to which indeed you were called in one body. And be thankful."

- Colossians 3:15, ESV.

Illustration: Imagine a pond where a single pebble is dropped. The ripples expand outward, touching every part. Gratitude has a similar effect, influencing not only our hearts but those around us.

Reflection and Insight: Expressing gratitude enriches our lives and can inspire and uplift others, creating a ripple effect.

Reflection Questions:

1. How has someone's gratitude positively affected you?

2. How can you create a ripple effect with your own gratitude?

_____

_____

_____

Call to Action: Express gratitude to someone who may not expect it and observe the positive effects.

Prayer and Reflection: Heavenly Father, let my gratitude touch not only my heart but also the hearts of those around me. Amen

DAY 44

Visual Day: Images of Joy

Guidance: Seek out images or scenes in your environment that elicit feelings of joy and gratitude. This could be a child's laughter, a sunrise, or a kind gesture from a stranger.

Reflection: Reflect on these visuals and consider how they remind us of God's constant blessings in our lives.

_____

_____

_____

Prayer: Lord, let me recognize and cherish the myriad ways You bring joy and gratitude into my life daily. Amen.

DAY 45

Feedback Day: Reflection on Gratitude

Guidance: Reflect on the past week. Consider the lessons learned, moments of gratitude, and how your perspective may have shifted.

Reflection Questions:

1. What was the most impactful lesson on gratitude for you this week?

2. How will you continue to cultivate a grateful heart?

_____

_____

_____

Prayer and Reflection: God, I thank You for this week of introspection and learning. May the seeds of gratitude planted grow and bear fruit in my life. Amen.

7

Service And Selflessness

This period is about the noble virtues of service and selflessness. Through the ages, many spiritual traditions have heralded the act of giving as a pathway to true fulfillment.

This week is dedicated to understanding how selfless acts can elevate our thoughts and bring a richer sense of purpose to our lives, no matter how minor they seem. We'll journey through scriptural insights, showcasing servant leaders and emphasizing the deep joy and contentment derived from aiding others.

As we explore the balance between self-care and selflessness, remember: in the act of giving, we often receive far more than we ever imagined. Let's embrace this week with open hearts, ready to touch and transform lives, one compassionate gesture at a time.

DAY 46

Elevating Thought Through Giving

Daily Premise:

"Each of you should give what you have decided in your heart to give, not reluctantly or under compulsion, for God loves a cheerful giver."

–2 Corinthians 9:7, NIV.

Illustration: Despite having little, a humble man always shared with those in need. Over time, his village flourished, showing that through giving, one can uplift an entire community.

Reflection and Insight: True giving transcends the physical act; it's about elevating our thoughts and intentions and recognizing the interconnectedness of all.

Reflection Questions:

1. How do you feel when you give selflessly?
2. Can you recall a time when giving elevated your thoughts or emotions?

_____

_____

_____

Call to Action: Find an opportunity to give without expecting anything in return.

Prayer and Reflection: Dear Lord, guide me to give selflessly, elevating my thoughts and actions towards the well-being of others. Amen.

DAY 47

The Joy of Serving Others

Daily Premise:

"For even the Son of Man did not come to be served, but to serve, and to give his life as a ransom for many."

- Mark 10:45, NIV.

Illustration: A young woman spent her weekends volunteering at a local shelter. Over time, she realized she gained more joy from serving others than any other pursuit.

Reflection and Insight: Service is a pathway to joy. Through it, we connect deeply with others, reflecting God's love.

Reflection Questions:

1. How does serving others bring you joy?
2. What opportunities do you see to serve in your community?

_____

_____

_____

Call to Action: Commit to a day of service this week, big or small.

Prayer and Reflection: God, open my heart to the joy of service, letting me see Your face in those I serve. Amen.

DAY 48

Embracing Empathy

Daily Premise:

"Rejoice with those who rejoice; mourn with those who mourn."

- Romans 12:15, NIV.

Illustration: A man, feeling the weight of his neighbor's grief, sat beside him silently, offering his presence. His empathy was a balm, helping heal a wounded heart.

Reflection and Insight: Empathy is a bridge connecting hearts, enabling us to feel with others and resonate with God's compassion.

Reflection Questions:

1. When have you deeply felt empathy for someone?
2. How can practicing empathy impact your spiritual journey?

_____

_____

_____

Call to Action: Reach out to someone going through a challenging time and offer your empathetic presence.

Prayer and Reflection: Lord, instill in me a heart of empathy, reflecting Your boundless compassion. Amen.

DAY 49

Scriptural Examples of Servant Leaders

Daily Premise:

"Whoever wants to become great among you must be your servant."

- Matthew 20:26, NIV.

Illustration: Jesus washed His disciples' feet, an act of profound humility and service. His leadership was rooted in love and service, setting a timeless example.

Reflection and Insight: Scripture is filled with examples of servant leaders, reminding us that authentic leadership is anchored in humility and service.

Reflection Questions:

1. Which scriptural servant leaders inspire you the most?

2. How can you embody their qualities in your daily life?

_____

_____

_____

Call to Action: Reflect on Jesus' acts of service and find ways to emulate them in your interactions.

Prayer and Reflection: Father, guide me to lead with a servant's heart, following the examples set in Your holy scriptures. Amen.

DAY 50

The Balance of Self-care and Selflessness

Daily Premise:

"Love your neighbor as yourself."

- Mark 12:31, NIV.

Illustration: A mother, always tending to her family, one day felt overwhelmed. Taking time for herself, she found renewed energy to serve with love.

Reflection and Insight: Self-care isn't selfish. By rejuvenating ourselves, we are better equipped to serve others with love and energy.

Reflection Questions:

1. How do you balance self-care with serving others?

2. When was the last time you took a moment for yourself?

_____

_____

_____

Call to Action: Carve out time this week specifically for self-care.

Prayer and Reflection: God, help me balance caring for myself and selflessly serving others. Amen.

DAY 51

Touching Lives, One Act at a Time

Daily Premise:

"Do not neglect to do good and to share what you have, for such sacrifices are pleasing to God."

- Hebrews 13:16, ESV.

Illustration: A small gesture, like a smile or a kind word, can change someone's day. No matter how small, each act has the power to touch lives.

Reflection and Insight: Every act of kindness, no matter its size, can create ripples of positivity in the world.

Reflection Questions:

1. How have small acts of kindness impacted you?

2. How can you touch lives through simple actions today?

_____

_____

_____

Call to Action: Perform a random act of kindness today.

Prayer and Reflection: Heavenly Father, guide me to touch lives through my daily acts, reflecting Your love. Amen.

DAY 52

Meditation Day: Compassionate Intention

Guidance:

1. Sit in a quiet space.

2. Focus on your breath.

3. Visualize compassion flowing from you, touching everyone you meet.

Reflection: Ponder on the interconnectedness of all beings and the role of compassion in bridging hearts.

_____

_____

_____

Prayer: Lord, let my intentions be rooted in compassion, connecting me deeper to others and You. Amen.

8

Mindfulness And Presence

The art of mindfulness and the beauty of being truly present. In our fast-paced world, it's easy to become trapped in the whirlwind of distractions, losing sight of the here and now.

This week aims to guide you back to the present moment, teaching you to cultivate a continuous awareness and find solace in stillness. By embracing mindfulness, you'll discover a more profound connection with the world around you and your innermost self.

We'll delve into scriptural perspectives, explore the mental benefits of living in the now, and celebrate the tranquility of genuine presence. Prepare to immerse yourself in the profound peace when we pause, breathe, and be.

DAY 53

The Art of Being Present

Daily Premise:

"Be present in all things and thankful for all things."

- Maya Angelou.

Illustration: In a busy marketplace, amidst the noise, a monk stood still, absorbing every sound, every movement, truly being present.

Reflection and Insight: Being present means fully engaging with the in the current moment, freeing oneself from distractions of the past or future.

Reflection Questions:

1. When do you find it most challenging to be present?

2. How can mindfulness practices improve your day-to-day life?

_____

_____

_____

Call to Action: Practice being present during a routine task today.

Prayer and Reflection: God, grant me the stillness to be truly present, cherishing each moment You provide. Amen.

DAY 54

Navigating Distractions

Daily Premise:

"Look straight ahead, and fix your eyes on what lies before you."

- Proverbs 4:25, NLT.

Illustration: A writer, amidst city noise, learned to focus on his work, navigating distractions by grounding himself in his passion.

Reflection and Insight: Distractions are inevitable. Navigating them requires mindfulness and a keen sense of purpose.

Reflection Questions:

1. What are your most frequent distractions?
2. How can you better navigate them to maintain focus?

_____

_____

_____

Call to Action: Set a designated quiet time, free from devices, to focus on a task.

Prayer and Reflection: Lord, guide me in focusing on what truly matters and navigating distractions with grace. Amen.

DAY 55

Embracing the Moment, Scripturally

Daily Premise:

"Therefore do not worry about tomorrow, for tomorrow will worry about itself. "

- Matthew 6:34, NIV.

Illustration: A farmer, not worried about the next harvest, enjoying the beauty of today, understanding the essence of embracing the moment.

Reflection and Insight: Scripture reminds us to be in the moment, trusting that God has a plan.

Reflection Questions:

1. How does scripture guide you in embracing the moment?

2. How can you apply this guidance today?

_____

_____

_____

Call to Action: Find a scriptural passage that reminds you to be in the present and meditate on it.

Prayer and Reflection: God, anchor me in the present, trusting in Your divine plan for the future. Amen.

DAY 56

The Mental Benefits of Mindfulness

Daily Premise:

"The present moment is filled with joy and happiness. If you are attentive, you will see it."

- Thich Nhat Hanh.

Illustration: A therapist introduced mindfulness to a stressed client. Over time, the client felt more at peace, highlighting the mental benefits of mindfulness.

Reflection and Insight: Mindfulness promotes mental clarity, reduces stress, and can improve emotional well-being.

Reflection Questions:

1. How has mindfulness positively impacted your mental well-being?

2. What mindfulness techniques resonate with you?

_____

_____

_____

Call to Action: Practice a 5-minute mindfulness meditation today.

Prayer and Reflection: Dear Lord, guide me towards mindfulness, enhancing my mental clarity and peace. Amen.

DAY 57

Cultivating Continuous Awareness

Daily Premise:

"The key to growth is the introduction of higher dimensions of consciousness into our awareness."

- Lao Tzu.

Illustration: A painter, always observant, saw beauty in every detail, showcasing the art of continuous awareness.

Reflection and Insight: Cultivating continuous awareness enhances our perceptions, allowing us to see the world more vibrantly.

Reflection Questions:

1. How do you cultivate continuous awareness in daily life?

2. How has this awareness enriched your experiences?

_____

_____

_____

Call to Action: Take a mindful walk, observing every detail around you.

Prayer and Reflection: God open my eyes to the world's intricacies, cultivating continuous awareness in me. Amen.

DAY 58

Celebrating Silence in a Noisy World

Daily Premise:

"Silence is a source of great strength."

- Lao Tzu.

Illustration: In a bustling city, a woman found solace in a silent rooftop garden, cherishing the strength silence provided.

Reflection and Insight: In a world full of noise, silence offers a refreshing reprieve, grounding us and renewing our spirits.

Reflection Questions:

1. How do you find pockets of silence in your daily life?

2. How does silence impact your mental and spiritual well-being?

_____

_____

_____

Call to Action: Dedicate 10 minutes today to sit in silence, disconnecting from the world's noise.

Prayer and Reflection: Lord, in the midst of life's noise, lead me to silence, rejuvenating my soul. Amen.

DAY 59

Visual Day: Peaceful Scenes of Stillness

Guidance: Gaze upon serene images of nature - a calm lake, towering mountains, or a tranquil forest. Absorb the stillness they project.

Reflection: Contemplate the peace that nature provides and how you can cultivate that same peace internally.

Prayer: God, let me find stillness in my heart, reflecting the peace I see in Your creation. Amen.

_____

_____

_____

DAY 60

Feedback Day: Reflection on Mindfulness

Guidance: Review the week's learnings on mindfulness. Reflect on the changes you've observed in your mental state and overall well-being.

Reflection Questions:

1. Which topic resonated the most with you this week?

2. How will you continue to integrate mindfulness into your life?

_____

_____

_____

Call to Action: Share your insights and experiences of this week with a friend or in your journal.

Prayer and Reflection: Lord, as I journey towards greater mindfulness, guide me and ground me in Your presence. Amen.

9

Wisdom And Learning

Dive into a world where wisdom intertwines with the joy of discovery. Wisdom isn't just about age or experience; it's a pursuit, an ongoing quest that thrives on curiosity and openness.

This week, we're taking you on an exploration of the wonders of lifelong learning and the profound depths of scriptural insights. Let's cherish the lessons from our past mistakes, find inspiration from venerable mentors, and ignite our innate sense of wonder. Embrace each day as a new opportunity to grow, question, and learn.

Welcome to a week of enlightenment and revelation. Let the journey to wisdom begin!

DAY 61

Valuing Lifelong Learning

Daily Premise:

"For the Lord gives wisdom; from his mouth come knowledge and understanding."

- Proverbs 2:6, NIV.

Illustration: A grandfather, at 80, took a pottery class, proving that the quest for knowledge knows no age.

Reflection and Insight: Embracing learning at every stage enriches life and keeps the mind agile.

Reflection Questions:

1. What new skills or knowledge have you recently acquired?

2. How do you maintain your zest for learning?

_____

_____

_____

Call to Action: Pick a book or online course on an unfamiliar topic and start today.

Prayer and Reflection: Lord, guide me to thirst for knowledge and understanding throughout my life. Amen.

DAY 62

Gaining Wisdom from Mistakes

Daily Premise:

"For though the righteous fall seven times, they rise again."

- Proverbs 24:16, NIV.

Illustration: Thomas Edison, after many failed attempts at inventing the light bulb, remarked that he didn't fail but found 10,000 ways that didn't work.

Reflection and Insight: Mistakes are not setbacks; they are stepping stones to wisdom.

Reflection Questions:

1. Can you recall a mistake that later turned into a learning opportunity?

2. How do you handle failures and setbacks?

_____

_____

_____

Call to Action: Reflect on a recent mistake and extract a learning lesson from it.

Prayer and Reflection: Lord, help me see my mistakes as opportunities to grow in wisdom and character. Amen.

DAY 63

Scriptural Insights on Wisdom

Daily Premise:

"The beginning of wisdom is this: Get wisdom. Though it cost all you have, get understanding."

- Proverbs 4:7, NIV.

Illustration: Ancient civilizations would send their young to learn from the elders, understanding that with age comes wisdom.

Reflection and Insight: Scripture places a high value on wisdom, urging us to seek it above all else.

Reflection Questions:

1. How do you actively seek wisdom in your daily life?
2. In what areas do you need divine wisdom the most?

_____

_____

_____

Call to Action: Take a moment today to seek advice or guidance from someone you consider wise.

Prayer and Reflection: Lord, lead me to Your wisdom and grant me the understanding I seek. Amen.

DAY 64

Mentors and Models in Elevating Thought

Daily Premise:

"We all need someone who inspires us to do better than we know how."

- Anonymous.

Illustration: Sir Isaac Newton once said, "If I have seen further, it is by standing on the shoulders of giants." This highlights the importance of mentors in our lives.

Reflection and Insight: Mentors provide guidance, wisdom, and insight, often elevating our perspectives.

Reflection Questions:

1. Who are the mentors in your life?
2. How have they shaped your thoughts and actions?

_____

_____

_____

Call to Action: Reach out to someone you consider a mentor and express gratitude.

Prayer and Reflection: Lord, thank You for placing mentors in my life to guide and uplift me. Amen.

DAY 65

Embracing Curiosity and Wonder

Daily Premise:

"Ask, and it will be given to you; seek, and you will find; knock, and the door will be opened to you."

– Matthew 7:7, NIV.

Illustration: A child, filled with wonder, gazes at the stars, imagining the vastness of the universe.

Reflection and Insight: Maintaining a sense of curiosity keeps our spirits alive and our minds active.

Reflection Questions:

1. What fills you with wonder?

2. How do you keep your sense of curiosity alive?

_____

_____

_____

Call to Action: Today, ask a question about something you've always wondered about.

Prayer and Reflection: Lord, reignite my sense of wonder and curiosity about Your magnificent creation. Amen.

DAY 66

The Power of Questions in Growth

Daily Premise:

"The important thing is not to stop questioning. Curiosity has its own reason for existing."

- Albert Einstein.

Illustration: Socrates taught his students to think critically and seek the truth through his method of questioning.

Reflection and Insight: Questions lead to answers, growth, and a deeper understanding of life.

Reflection Questions:

1. What powerful questions have you asked recently?

2. How have questions led to personal growth in your life?

_____

_____

_____

Call to Action: Challenge yourself to ask more profound questions in your conversations today.

Prayer and Reflection: Lord, inspire me to seek answers and grow through my questions. Amen.

DAY 67

Meditation Day: Seeking Divine Wisdom

Daily Premise:

"If any of you lacks wisdom, you should ask God, who gives generously to all without finding fault, and it will be given to you."

- James 1:5, NIV.

Guided Reflection: Close your eyes. Imagine yourself in a vast library filled with books of wisdom. God is there, inviting you to ask anything. What would you ask for? Envision receiving that wisdom.

Reflection Questions:

1. What areas in your life require divine wisdom?

2. How does meditation help you connect with the wisdom of God?

_____

_____

_____

Call to Action: Set aside 10 minutes today for quiet meditation, seeking divine guidance.

Prayer and Reflection: Lord, grant me the wisdom I seek and guide my thoughts in alignment with Your will. Amen.

10

Balance And Harmony

S tep into a realm where equilibrium reigns supreme, where the rhythm of life dances in perfect harmony. Balance is not just a state but an art, a delicate blend of embracing life's highs and lows.

This week guides you through the scriptural insights on balance, teaches you to find peace amidst the storms, and inspires you to harmonize your mind, body, and spirit. Life, with all its seasons, beckons you to find your center.

So, let's embark on this journey to achieve that inner serenity and embrace the symphony of life. Dive in and let the harmonious transformation unfold!

DAY 68

Achieving Mental and Spiritual Equilibrium

Daily Premise:

-"*Let your moderation be known unto all men. The Lord is at hand.*"

Philippians 4:5, KJV.

Illustration: A tightrope walker maintains balance by focusing on a fixed point ahead, much like we can focus on our spiritual center amidst life's challenges.

Reflection and Insight: Finding equilibrium in life requires us to center ourselves spiritually, mentally, and emotionally.

Reflection Questions:

1. How do you find your center when life becomes chaotic?

2. What practices help you maintain spiritual equilibrium?

_____

_____

_____

Call to Action: Dedicate a few moments today for deep breathing, envisioning peace and balance filling your body.

Prayer and Reflection: Lord, guide me to find balance and harmony in my daily life, anchoring my spirit in You. Amen.

DAY 69

Navigating Life's Ups and Downs

Daily Premise:

> *"When times are good, be happy; but when times are bad, consider this: God has made the one as well as the other."*

- Ecclesiastes 7:14, NIV.

Illustration: A roller coaster, with its highs and lows, mirrors the unpredictability and thrill of life.

Reflection and Insight: Embracing life's peaks and valleys allows us to experience its richness fully.

Reflection Questions:

1. How do you handle the highs and lows of life?

2. Can you recall a low point that later revealed itself as a blessing?

_____

_____

_____

Call to Action: Write down a challenge you're facing and three potential lessons or growth opportunities it presents.

Prayer and Reflection: Lord, give me the grace to navigate life's ups and downs with faith and resilience. Amen.

DAY 70

Scriptural Insights on Balance

Daily Premise:

"A false balance is an abomination to the LORD, but a just weight is his delight."

- Proverbs 11:1, ESV.

Illustration: Ancient merchants used balance scales to ensure fair trade, emphasizing the importance of balance in justice.

Reflection and Insight: In all aspects of life, balance is aligned with divine principles and leads to righteousness.

Reflection Questions:

1. How do you ensure balance in your relationships, work, and spiritual life?

2. Where in your life might you be leaning too heavily to one side?

_____

_____

_____

Call to Action: Reflect on one area of your life that needs more balance and set intentions to address it.

Prayer and Reflection: Lord, lead me to walk in balance, reflecting Your divine harmony in all I do. Amen.

DAY 71

Harmonizing Mind, Body, and Spirit

Daily Premise:

"Happiness is when what you think, what you say, and what you do are in harmony."

- Mahatma Gandhi.

Illustration: A symphony orchestra, with each instrument playing its part, creates a harmonious melody, representing the synchronicity of mind, body, and spirit.

Reflection and Insight: True harmony is achieved when our thoughts, actions, and spirit are aligned with our purpose and values.

Reflection Questions:

1. How do you cultivate harmony within yourself?
2. Are there any discordant areas in your life that need attention?

_____

_____

_____

Call to Action: Practice a short mindfulness exercise today, checking in with your thoughts, feelings, and physical sensations.

Prayer and Reflection: Lord, guide me to live in harmony, aligning my mind, body, and spirit with Your purpose. Amen.

DAY 72

Embracing Seasons of Life

Daily Premise:

"To everything, there is a season, and a time to every purpose under the heaven."

- Ecclesiastes 3:1, KJV.

Illustration: The ever-changing seasons – from the rebirth in spring to the dormancy of winter – remind us of life's cyclical nature.

Reflection and Insight: Life consists of seasons, each with its purpose and lessons.

Reflection Questions:

1. What season of life are you currently in?

2. How do you adapt and find joy in each season?

_____

_____

_____

Call to Action: Reflect on the current season of your life, noting its blessings and challenges.

Prayer and Reflection: Lord, grant me the grace to embrace each season of life with gratitude and hope. Amen.

DAY 73

Finding Peace Amidst Chaos

Daily Premise:

"In the midst of movement and chaos, keep stillness inside of you."

- Deepak Chopra.

Illustration: Amidst a bustling market, a monk sits in deep meditation, undisturbed by the surrounding chaos, symbolizing inner peace.

Reflection and Insight: Even in chaotic situations, it's possible to cultivate inner stillness and peace.

Reflection Questions:

1. How do you maintain inner calm amidst external chaos?

2. Can you recall a moment when you felt peaceful despite outer turmoil?

_____

_____

_____

Call to Action: Engage in a brief meditation session today, focusing on cultivating inner peace.

Prayer and Reflection: Lord, in the whirlwind of life, help me find a calm center rooted in You. Amen.

DAY 74

Visual Day: Symbols of Balance

Visual Prompt: View an image of the Yin and Yang symbol, representing balance and duality in ancient Chinese philosophy.

Guided Reflection: Consider the harmonious interaction of opposites in the symbol. Ponder on how areas of light and darkness in your life can coexist balanced.

Reflection Questions:

1. What does this symbol evoke in you regarding balance in your own life?

2. How can you integrate opposing forces in your life to create harmony?

_____

_____

_____

Call to Action: Sketch or find your own symbol of balance and place it where you can see it daily.

Prayer and Reflection: Lord, help me embrace the light and shadow within, guiding me towards a balanced existence. Amen.

DAY 75

Feedback Day: Reflection on Harmony

Guided Reflection: Look back over the past week. Reflect on moments when you felt in harmony and times when you felt out of sync.

Reflection Questions:

1. Which day's content resonated most with you this week?

2. How have your perceptions of balance and harmony shifted?

_____

_____

_____

Call to Action: Share your insights from this week with a friend or in your journal.

Prayer and Reflection: Lord, as I reflect on this week, guide me towards greater harmony in my life. Help me to carry these lessons forward. Amen.

11

Courage And Conviction

Get ready because this week is all about being brave and sticking to what you believe in! We will learn about incredible stories from scriptures that show how brave people can be. Plus, we'll talk about how to face tough times and not give up. By the end of this week, you'll feel stronger inside and ready to stand up for what's right. Let's dive in and find our inner heroes!

DAY 76

Braving the Unknown

Daily Premise:

"Have I not commanded you? Be strong and courageous. Do not be afraid; do not be discouraged, for the LORD your God will be with you wherever you go."

- Joshua 1:9, NIV.

Illustration: An explorer venturing into a dense forest, uncertain of what lies ahead but equipped with tools and determination.

Reflection and Insight: Venturing into the unfamiliar necessitates faith and courage. Yet, with God's guidance, we can overcome any obstacle.

Reflection Questions:

1. What unknowns are confronting you presently?
2. How does faith serve as your compass in ambiguous times?

_____

_____

_____

Call to Action: Spell out three life uncertainties and write a prayer or affirmation for each.

Prayer and Reflection: Lord, as I tread into the unfamiliar, consistently remind me of Your unwavering presence. Amen.

DAY 77

Standing Firm in Convictions

Daily Premise:

"Therefore, my dear brothers and sisters, stand firm. Let nothing move you."

- 1 Corinthians 15:58, NIV.

Illustration: A steadfast lighthouse amidst tempestuous seas, safely directing vessels.

Reflection and Insight: Our convictions serve as our guiding beacon. Demonstrating resilience by adhering to them even under duress showcases our integrity.

Reflection Questions:

1. Which convictions do you cherish?

2. Has there ever been a time when your beliefs wavered? What fortified your resolve?

_____

_____

_____

Call to Action: Reflect on an instance when you staunchly upheld your beliefs—document what fueled your perseverance.

Prayer and Reflection: Lord, bestow upon me the tenacity to unyieldingly uphold my convictions, even when the world challenges them. Amen.

DAY 78

Scriptural Teachings on Bravery

Daily Premise:

"The wicked flee though no one pursues, but the righteous are as bold as a lion."

- Proverbs 28:1, NIV.

Illustration: A lion leading its pride without fear, epitomizing courage and might.

Reflection and Insight: The Holy Scriptures counsel us that righteousness endows us with a form of formidable and enduring bravery.

Reflection Questions:

1. In what ways does scripture enhance your courage?

2. Which biblical character's bravery do you resonate with most?

_____

_____

_____

Call to Action: Dig into the narrative of a biblical personality renowned for their bravery. Highlight qualities you admire.

Prayer and Reflection: Lord, instill the lion's courage within me, grounded in Your Word and teachings. Amen.

DAY 79

The Mental Strength of Conviction

Daily Premise:

"Conviction is worth nothing unless it is converted into conduct."

- Thomas Carlyle.

Illustration: A sculptor meticulously carving a block, transmuting solid stone into art, driven by undeterred conviction.

Reflection and Insight: True conviction power resides in belief and manifests through our actions and behaviors.

Reflection Questions:

1. How have your convictions influenced your actions?

2. Can you pinpoint a time when your actions mirrored a profound belief?

_____

_____

_____

Call to Action: Identify an aspect of your life where actions could better reflect your convictions and strategize how to align them.

Prayer and Reflection: Lord, may my convictions be evident in thought and deed. Amen.

DAY 80

Facing Adversity with Grace

Daily Premise:

"But he said to me, 'My grace is sufficient for you, for my power is made perfect in weakness."

- 2 Corinthians 12:9, NIV.

Illustration: A tree, although swaying, remains unbroken against a tempest's might, epitomizing resilience and elegance.

Reflection and Insight: God's divine grace enables us to confront hardships with composure, emphasizing that His strength prevails in our vulnerabilities.

Reflection Questions:

1. In challenging moments, how has God's grace been your ally?

2. What does confronting adversity gracefully mean to you?

_____

_____

_____

Call to Action: Reflect upon a recent hardship. Draft a note of gratitude, recognizing the grace you perceived during that period.

Prayer and Reflection: Lord, even in my fragile moments, may Your grace be my guiding light, elevating and guiding me. Amen.

DAY 81

Overcoming Doubt with Determination

Daily Premise:

"I can do all things through Christ who strengthens me."

- Philippians 4:13, NKJV.

Illustration: A mountaineer ardently scaling a formidable peak, pushing doubts aside with eyes set on the summit.

Reflection and Insight: While doubts may sometimes obscure our journey, we can triumph over any impediment with unyielding determination and faith.

Reflection Questions:

1. How do you steer through moments riddled with doubt?

2. When shrouded in uncertainty, what fuels your drive to advance?

_____

_____

_____

Call to Action: Recognize a current doubt and meditate or pray on it, seeking divine direction and clarity.

Prayer and Reflection: Lord, in times of uncertainty, fortify my spirit with unwavering determination and faith. Amen.

DAY 82

Meditation Day: Cultivating Inner Strength

Daily Premise:

"He gives power to the weak, And to those who have no might He increases strength."

- Isaiah 40:29, NKJV.

Illustration: The deep roots of a tree, ensuring its robustness and stability, even in storms.

Reflection and Insight: Analogous to a tree's strength vested in its roots, our intrinsic might is fostered through profound reflection and a connection with the Divine.

Reflection Questions:

1. How do you nourish your inner fortitude?

2. Which rituals assist you in connecting profoundly with your spiritual essence?

Call to Action: Set aside 10 minutes today for a meditation session to visualize your inner vigor and resilience.

Prayer and Reflection: Lord, during today's meditation, guide me to tap into the boundless strength You've instilled within me. Amen.

12

Celebration And Conclusiveness

Guess what? We've made it to the last week! It's time to celebrate all we've learned and look back at our awesome journey. This week is like a big party for our minds and spirits. We'll also chat about how endings can lead to exciting new starts. So, let's wrap things up, cheer for our progress, and get pumped for what comes next!

DAY 83

Celebrating the Journey Thus Far

Daily Premise:

"Rejoice in the Lord always. I will say it again: Rejoice!"

- Philippians 4:4, NIV.

Illustration: A marathon runner pausing at a viewpoint, looking back at the trail behind, and appreciating the distance covered.

Reflection and Insight: Every step in our journey, no matter how challenging, contributes to our growth and should be celebrated.

Reflection Questions:

1. What moments from this journey stand out to you the most?

2. How have these moments shaped or changed you?

_____

_____

_____

Call to Action: Take a moment to write down three significant milestones you've achieved during this journey.

Prayer and Reflection: Lord, thank You for guiding me through this journey. Let me always find joy in every step. Amen.

DAY 84

Embracing New Beginnings

Daily Premise:

"Behold, I am doing a new thing; now it springs forth, do you not perceive it?"

- Isaiah 43:19, ESV.

Illustration: A sunrise over a calm sea, symbolizing new opportunities and fresh starts.

Reflection and Insight: As one chapter closes, God opens a new one filled with hope, promise, and potential.

Reflection Questions:

1. What new beginnings are you looking forward to?

2. How can you prepare yourself for these new opportunities?

_____

_____

_____

Call to Action: List three new things or changes you'd like to embrace going forward.

Prayer and Reflection: Lord, as one chapter closes, prepare my heart for the new beginnings that You have in store. Amen.

DAY 85

Scriptural Reflections on Completion

Daily Premise:

"I have fought the good fight, I have finished the race, I have kept the faith."

- 2 Timothy 4:7, NIV.

Illustration: A builder placing the final brick on a structure, marking its completion.

Reflection and Insight: Completing our tasks with dedication and faith ensures we finish strong and aligned with God's will.

Reflection Questions:

1. How do you feel about reaching this point in your journey?

2. What does completion mean to you in a spiritual context?

_____

_____

_____

Call to Action: Reflect on the lessons and growth you've experienced, cherishing the sense of completion.

Prayer and Reflection: Lord, thank You for the strength to see things through. Help me to always finish the race with You by my side. Amen.

DAY 86

Preparing for Your Next Chapter

Daily Premise:

"The future belongs to those who believe in the beauty of their dreams."

- Eleanor Roosevelt.

Illustration: A sailor charting a new course on a map, ready to embark on another voyage.

Reflection and Insight: Every ending is a new beginning. Preparing with hope and optimism ensures a journey aligned with our dreams.

Reflection Questions:

1. What are your hopes for the next chapter of your journey?

2. How will you prepare for what's next?

_____

_____

_____

Call to Action: Write down three goals you wish to achieve in the next chapter of your journey.

Prayer and Reflection: Lord, guide me as I prepare for my next life phase. May my path align with Your purpose. Amen.

DAY 87

Acknowledging Transformations

Daily Premise:

"Do not be conformed to this world, but be transformed by the renewal of your mind."

- Romans 12:2, ESV.

Illustration: A caterpillar's transformation into a butterfly symbolizes growth and change.

Reflection and Insight: Throughout our journey, inner transformations align us more closely with God's purpose.

Reflection Questions:

1. In what ways have you transformed during this journey?
2. What internal changes are you most proud of?

_____

_____

_____

Call to Action: Reflect, acknowledge, and appreciate the changes.

Prayer and Reflection: Lord, thank You for the transformations in my life. Continue to mold me in Your image. Amen.

DAY 88

Visual Day: Celebratory Images

Image Description: A group of diverse individuals releasing colorful balloons into a clear blue sky.

Reflection: Each balloon represents individual achievements, challenges overcome, and moments of growth. Releasing them signifies offering our gratitude to God and celebrating the journey.

Reflection Questions:

1. What emotions does this image evoke in you?

2. How do you visualize your personal celebrations?

_____

_____

_____

Call to Action: Find or create a visual representation of your journey's celebrations and share it with someone close.

Prayer and Reflection: Lord, may I always find reasons to celebrate in the blessings You bestow upon me. Amen.

DAY 89

Feedback Day: Final Reflections

Daily Premise:

"Feedback is the breakfast of champions."

- Ken Blanchard.

Illustration: A potter refining a clay vessel based on its initial shape, symbolizing the importance of reflection and feedback.

Reflection and Insight: Taking time to reflect on our journey and seeking feedback allows for continuous growth and improvement.

Reflection Questions:

1. What insights have you gained from reflecting on your journey?

2. How can feedback from others enhance your growth?

_____

_____

_____

Call to Action: Seek feedback from a trusted individual about your journey and growth during this period.

Prayer and Reflection: Lord, grant me the wisdom to learn from reflection and feedback, always striving to grow closer to You. Amen.

DAY 90

Closing Thoughts and Forward Momentum

Daily Premise:

"But grow in the grace and knowledge of our Lord and Savior Jesus Christ. To him be the glory both now and to the day of eternity."

–2 Peter 3:18, ESV.

Illustration: A traveler at a crossroads, looking forward with determination, ready for the journey ahead.

Reflection and Insight: As we conclude this leg of the journey, we must keep moving forward with grace, knowledge, and faith in God's plan.

Reflection Questions:

1. How has this journey prepared you for the future?

2. What are your aspirations moving forward?

_____

_____

_____

Call to Action: Write a letter to your future self, capturing your feelings, lessons learned, and hopes for the next phase.

Prayer and Reflection: Lord, as I move forward, keep me anchored in Your grace and wisdom. Guide my steps always. Amen.

Congratulations on closing this phase of your journey. I pray you have found this devotional both enlightening and thought-provoking. You are now aware of the power of reframing your reality and elevating your thinking. Remember, this awareness is the first step towards a transformative journey. Embrace it with hope and determination. Commit to cultivating positive thoughts, seeking guidance through prayer and meditation, and embracing your limitless potential.

Choose to reframe your reality by elevating your thinking. Keep elevating and growing, and watch your journey unfold with joy, peace, and fulfillment.

www.ingramcontent.com/pod-product-compliance
Lightning Source LLC
Chambersburg PA
CBHW071516120626
46550CB00006B/2251